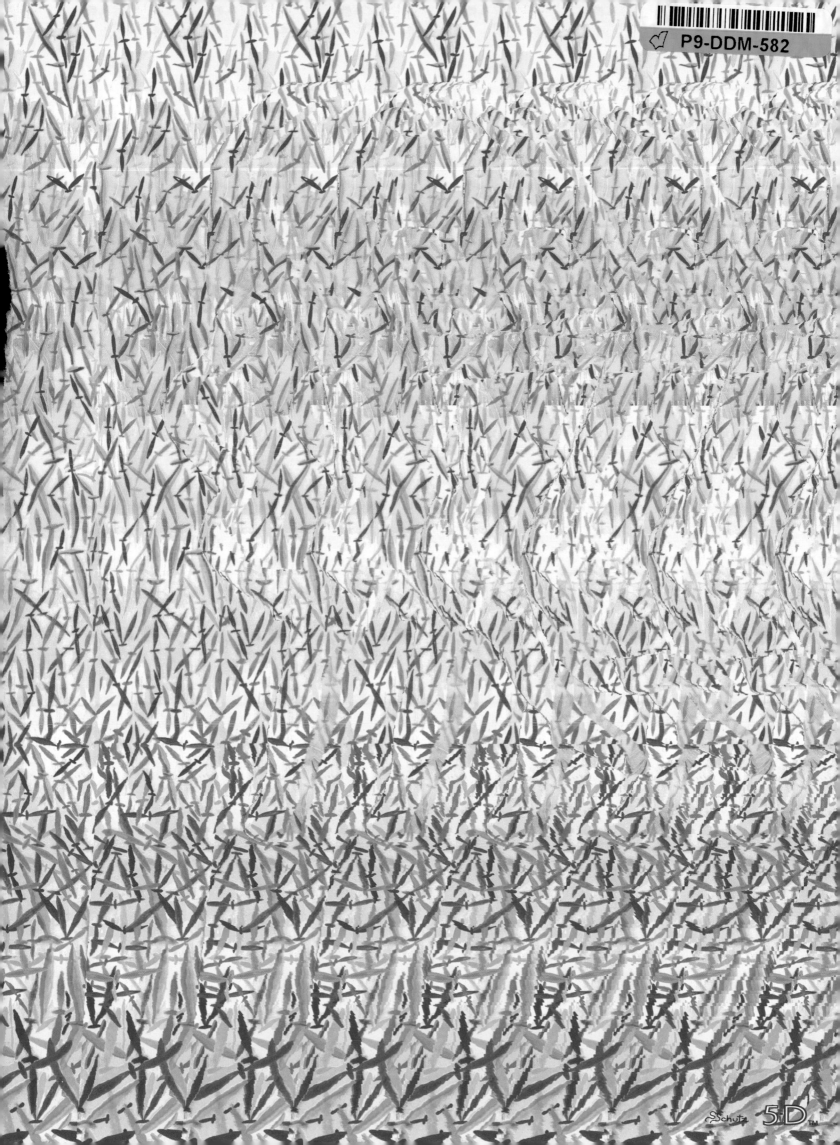

Schutz 5.D™

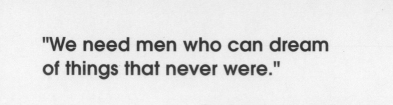

"We need men who can dream
of things that never were."

President John F. Kennedy

"Oh, Say Can You See Liberty in 3-D? For some, computers give a third dimension... At times a little yelp of excitement is heard."

— John Burgess, *The Washington Post*

"Over the past few years, random-dot stereograms have been popping up all over the place. Unfortunately, most are very boring. Well, this has all changed with the release of the Blue Mountain Arts 5-D_{TM} stereograms developed by Dr. Stephen Schutz. In their flat format, they are works of art in their own right. When viewed in three dimensions, you will be amazed and delighted with the clarity and ingenious blending of theme. No more patterns of endless dots. Every Blue Mountain Arts print is a blend of familiar objects or pleasing geometric patterns, and the 3-D image you will soon see is sure to delight. But be forewarned, this will be habit-forming, and you will be begging Blue Mountain Arts® to come out with more, more, and more."

— Sheldon Aronowitz
Writer, *Stereo World* magazine,
and Owner of the largest 3-D
collection in the world

"Blue Mountain Arts of Boulder, Colorado, exploded out of the gates with... 5-D_{TM} stereograms. Blue Mountain Arts... is the creation of the husband and wife team, Stephen Schutz, who combined an interest in art with a doctorate in theoretical physics, and Susan Polis Schutz, a widely published author of love poetry."

— Steve Woodward, *The Oregonian*

"In high-emotion... the reigning star is Susan Polis Schutz."

—TIME

*How to see the hidden 5-D_{TM} stereogram image:
Read instructions on next page.*

What is a 5-D™ stereogram?

A stereogram is a computer-generated image that "pops out" of the paper as if it were a Multi-Dimensional object. In order to see this image, however, the stereogram must be viewed in a certain way.

In the 1950s, people wore red and green glasses to see movies and pictures in 3-D. In 1960, Bela Julesz at Bell Laboratories invented the random-dot stereogram, which enabled people to see 3-D images without special glasses by taking advantage of the way our brain interprets depth.

Dr. Stephen Schutz, artist and physicist, recently pioneered a new technique and authored a program that produces Multi-Dimensional images from real artwork rather than from random dots. By removing the random dots from stereograms, Dr. Schutz has raised the art of the stereogram to a new level of aesthetic beauty — the 5-D™ stereogram.

Each page of artwork in this book has a hidden Multi-Dimensional image waiting to be discovered by you. Just follow the directions below, and you will experience a truly astounding form of interactive art.

How to see the hidden 5-D™ stereogram image:

Hold the art close to your nose so that it appears blurry. Relax and stare at it. Make believe you are looking "through" the art. Slowly move it away from your face until an image "pops out" and becomes perfectly clear. The time it takes to see the image can vary, so don't get discouraged!

Alternate viewing method: Place a sheet of plastic or glass over the page so that you can see your own reflection. Hold the art at arm's length and focus on your reflection in the plastic or glass until the 5-D™ stereogram image begins to "pop out."

Important: If you experience any discomfort, then stop, rest, and try again later.

Reach for Your Dreams in 5-D™ Stereograms

Contains Amazing Hidden Multi-Dimensional Images

Created by Stephen Schutz, Ph.D., and Susan Polis Schutz

Each page of artwork in this book has a hidden 5-D™ stereogram picture waiting to be discovered by you.
But first, please read the directions on the facing page.

Blue Mountain Press ®

Boulder, Colorado

Mail Order

Most of the 5-D™ stereograms published in this book are available on greeting cards, prints, and calendars.

Due to the enormous popularity of Blue Mountain Arts' products, you may find that your local stores are temporarily out of the designs you desire. If this should happen, we welcome your mail-order inquiries.

Write to us for information:

Blue Mountain Arts, Inc.
Mail Order
P.O. Box 4549
Boulder, CO 80306
(303) 449-0536

5-D is a trademark of Blue Mountain Arts, Inc.

The following people are to be thanked for their valuable contribution to this book: Faith Gowan, Jody Kauflin, Norine Neely, Jan Betts, Doug Pagels, John Crane, Patty Brown, Ed Guzik, Mark Rinella, Matt Rantanen, and Jared Schutz.

Thanks to the Hollywood Chamber of Commerce for use of the Hollywood sign that appears in the 5-D™ stereogram "Hollywood Stars." TM/© 1994 Hollywood Chamber of Commerce under license authorized by Curtis Management Group, Indianapolis, Indiana 46202 USA.

Thanks to *The Washington Post* for use of the quotes by John Burgess. © 1994 *The Washington Post*. Reprinted with permission.

ISBN: 0-88396-388-4
Library of Congress Catalog Card Number: 94-20653

Library of Congress Cataloging-in-Publication Data

Schutz, Stephen.
    Reach for your dreams in 5-D™ stereograms/
created by Stephen Schutz and Susan Polis Schutz.
        p.   cm.
    "Contains hidden multidimensional image art."
    ISBN 0-88396-388-4 : $17.95
    1. Schutz, Stephen. 2. Computer art — United States. 3. Optical
illusions in art. 4. American poetry — 20th century. I. Schutz, Susan
Polis. II. Title.
N7433.85.S38A4 1994
760—dc20   94-20653
                                                                  CIP

Printed in Hong Kong
First Printing: June, 1994

Blue Mountain Press ®

P.O. Box 4549, Boulder, Colorado 80306

Introduction

Everyone has dreams. Some people dream of freedom; some of peace. Some people dream of love; some of success. Some people dream about happiness; some about the intrinsic qualities needed to attain happiness.

Reach for Your Dreams in 5-D$_{TM}$ *Stereograms* represents the American Dream. What do we want for ourselves? What do we want for others? What do we dream about to make the world a better place?

Reach for Your Dreams in 5-D$_{TM}$ *Stereograms* contains the dreams that Stephen and I reach for. In the true spirit of innovation and inventiveness, our book utilizes a phenomenal art form created by Stephen Schutz: the 5-D$_{TM}$ stereogram. Stephen's sensitive graphics, with meaningful hidden images, bring the craft of the stereogram to a new level of aesthetic beauty.

We hope *Reach for Your Dreams in 5-D*$_{TM}$ *Stereograms* encourages you to explore your dreams.

"Only you can take the power
to make your dreams
come true"

Susan Polis Schutz

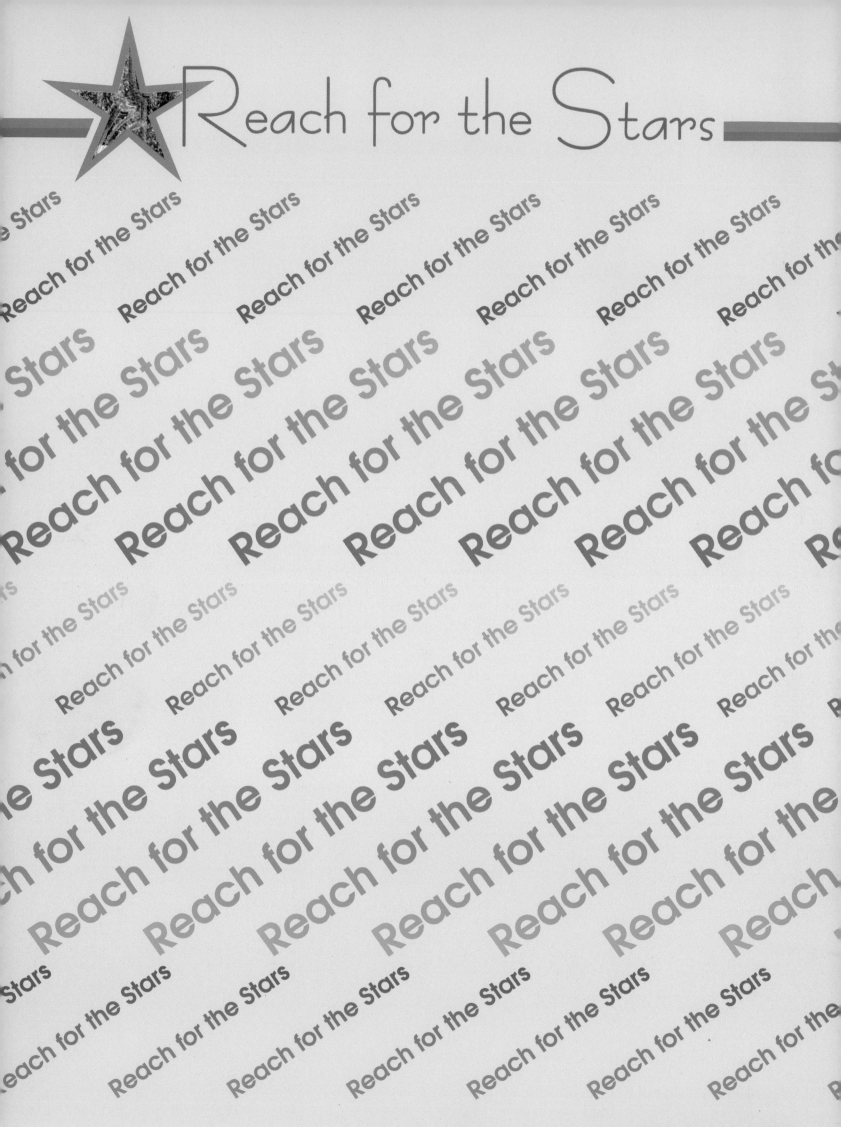

5-D™ Stereogram Image: **"Hollywood Stars"**

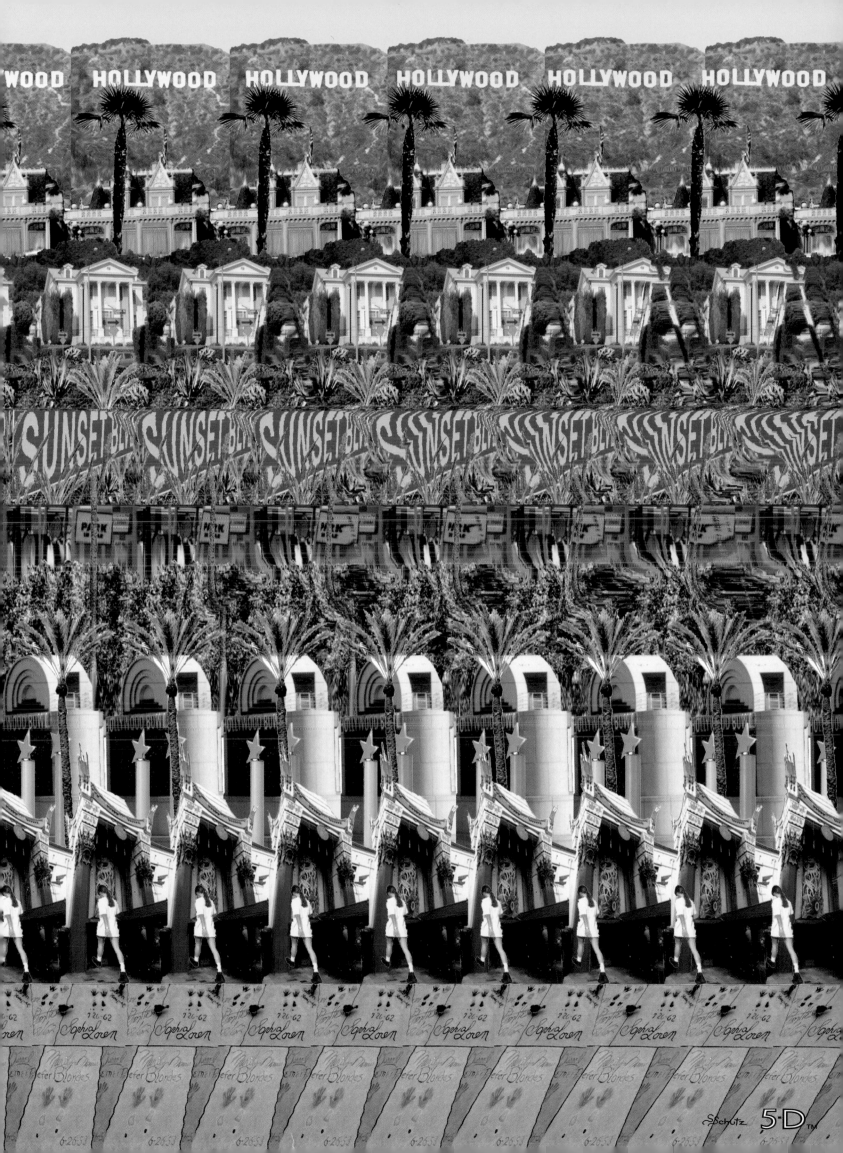

5-D™ Stereogram Image: **"Basketball Player"**

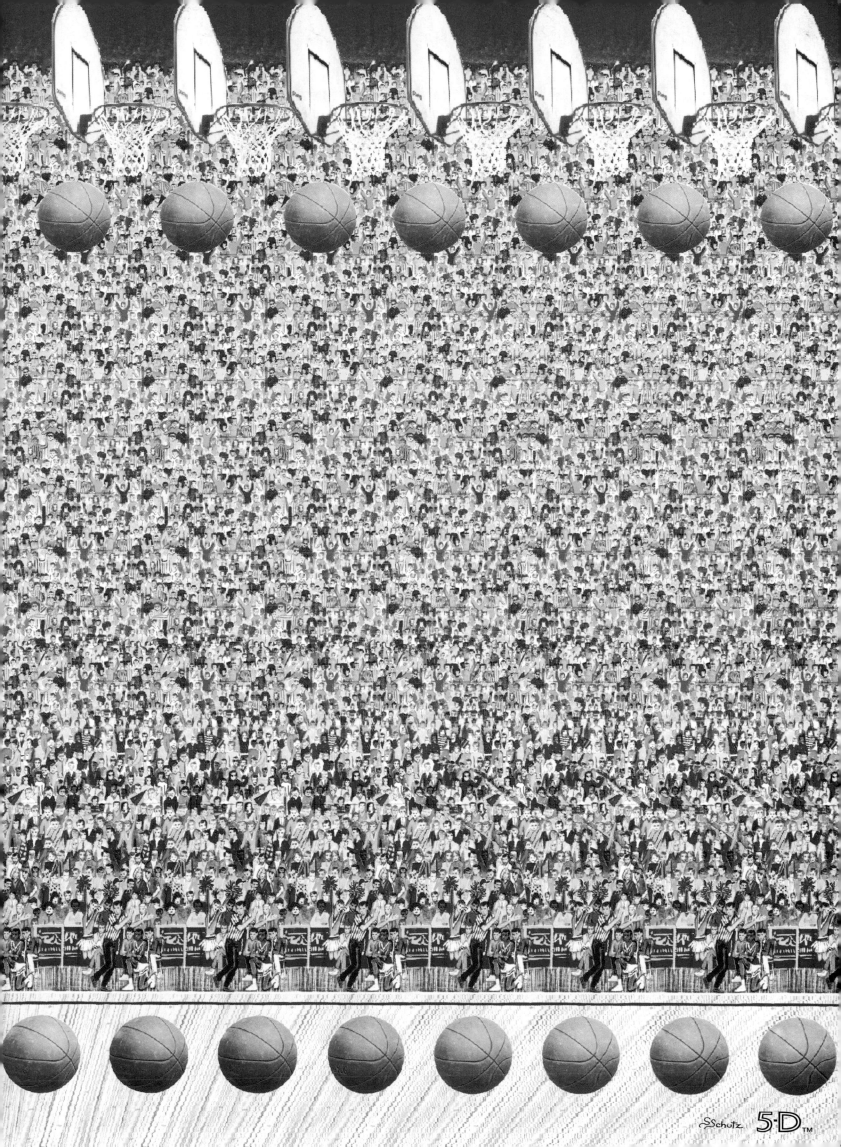

Nature

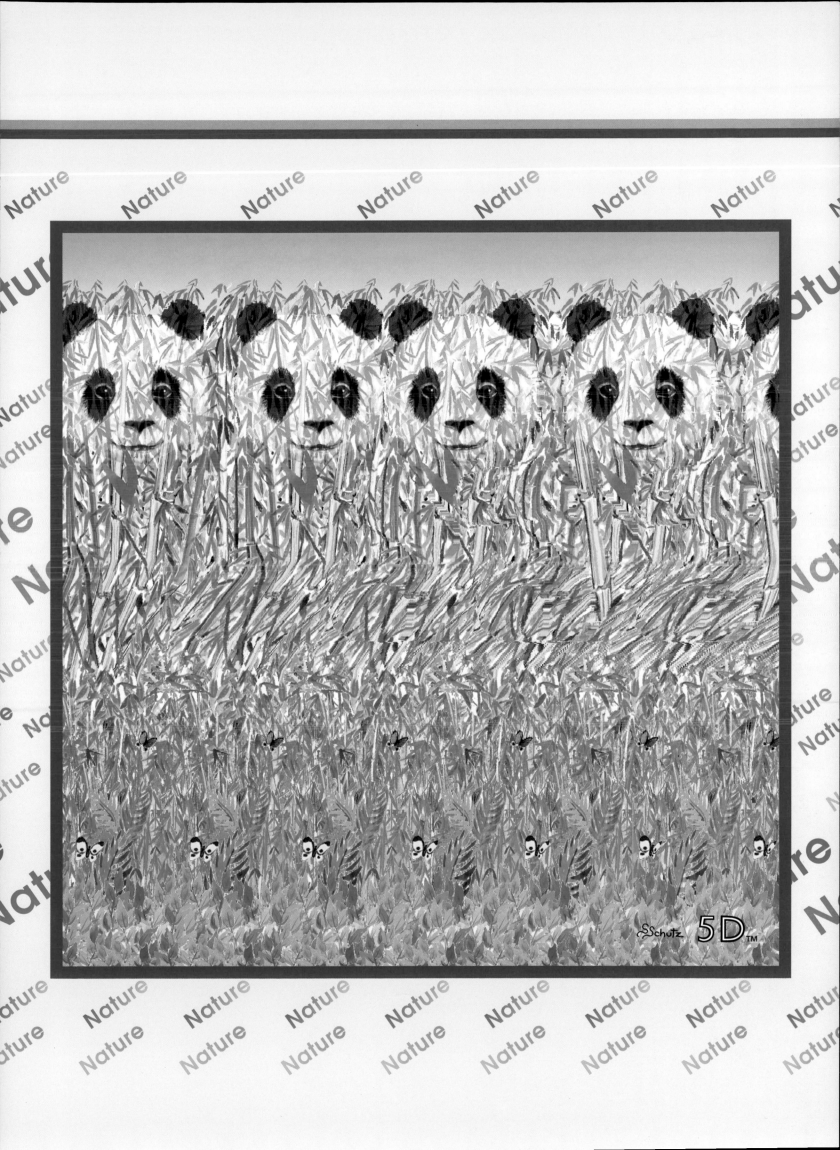

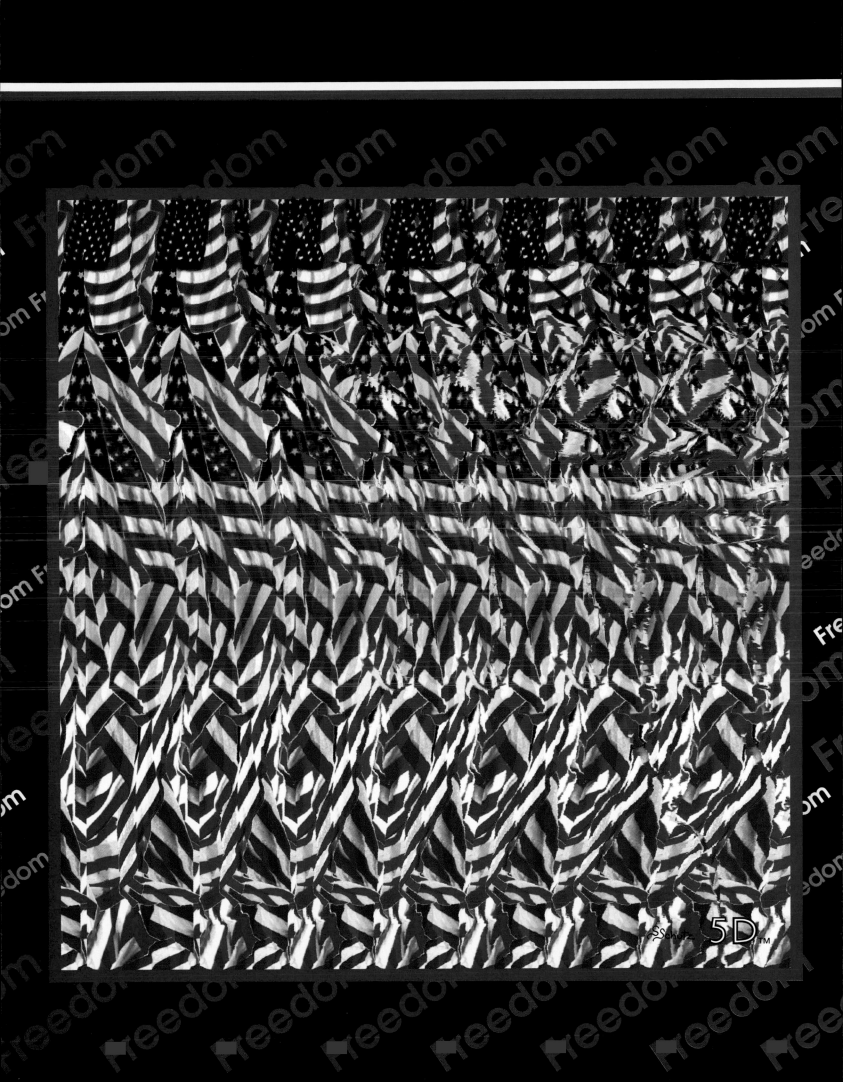

Harmony

5-D™ Stereogram Image: **"Bald Eagle over Grand Canyon"**

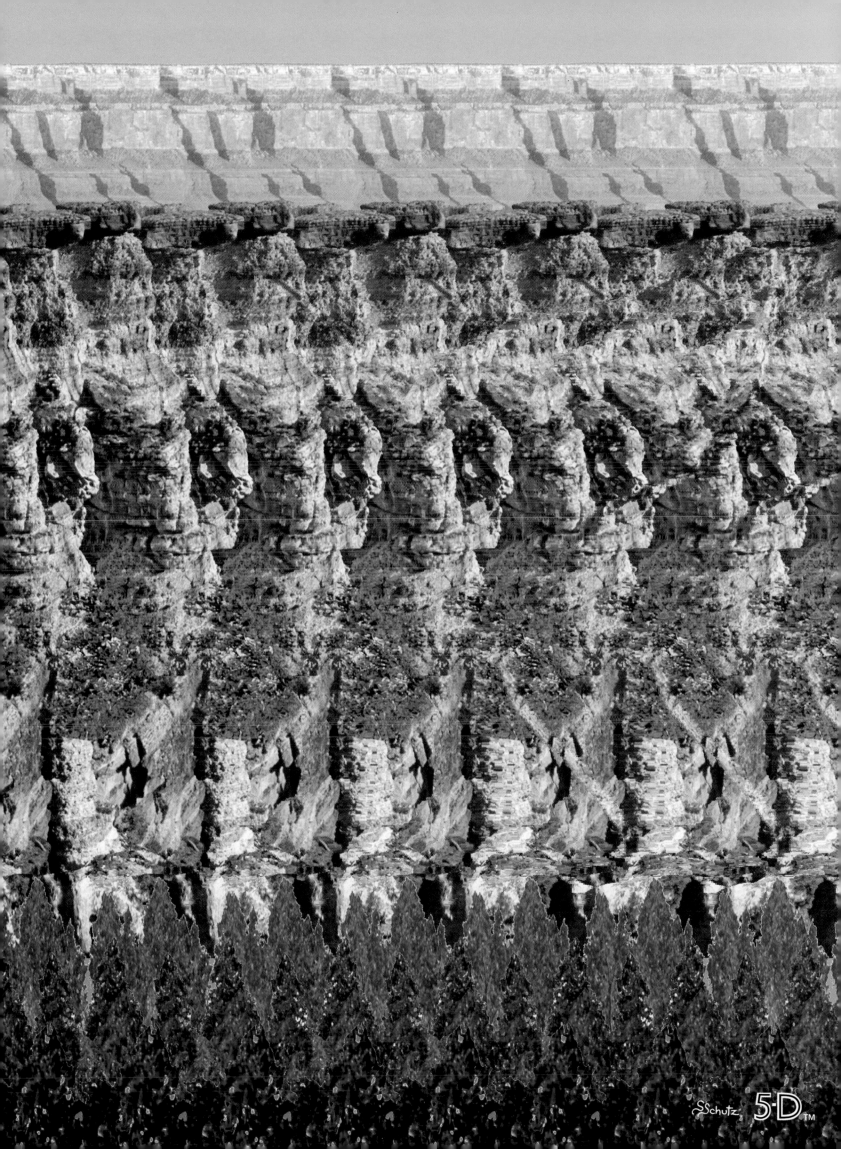

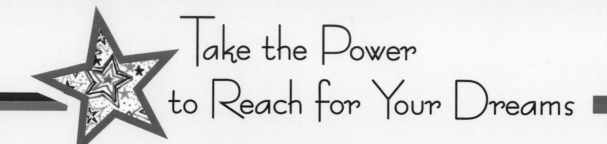

Take the Power to Reach for Your Dreams

This life is yours
Take the power
to choose what you want to do
and do it well
Take the power
to love what you want in life
and love it honestly
Take the power
to walk in the forest
and be a part of nature
Take the power
to control your own life
No one else can do it for you
Nothing is too good for you
You deserve the best
Take the power
to make your life
healthy
exciting
worthwhile
and very happy
Take the power
to reach for your dreams

- Susan Polis Schutz

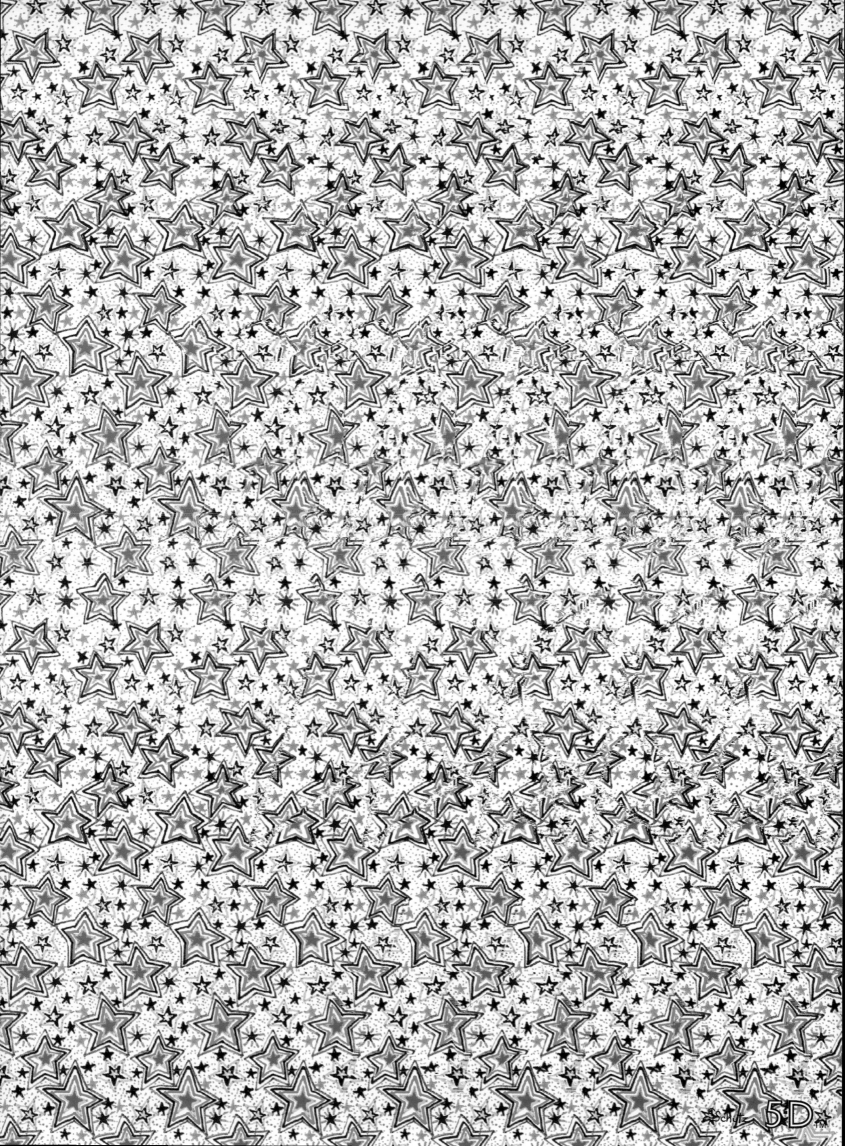

Confidence

Fun, Enjoyment, Excitement

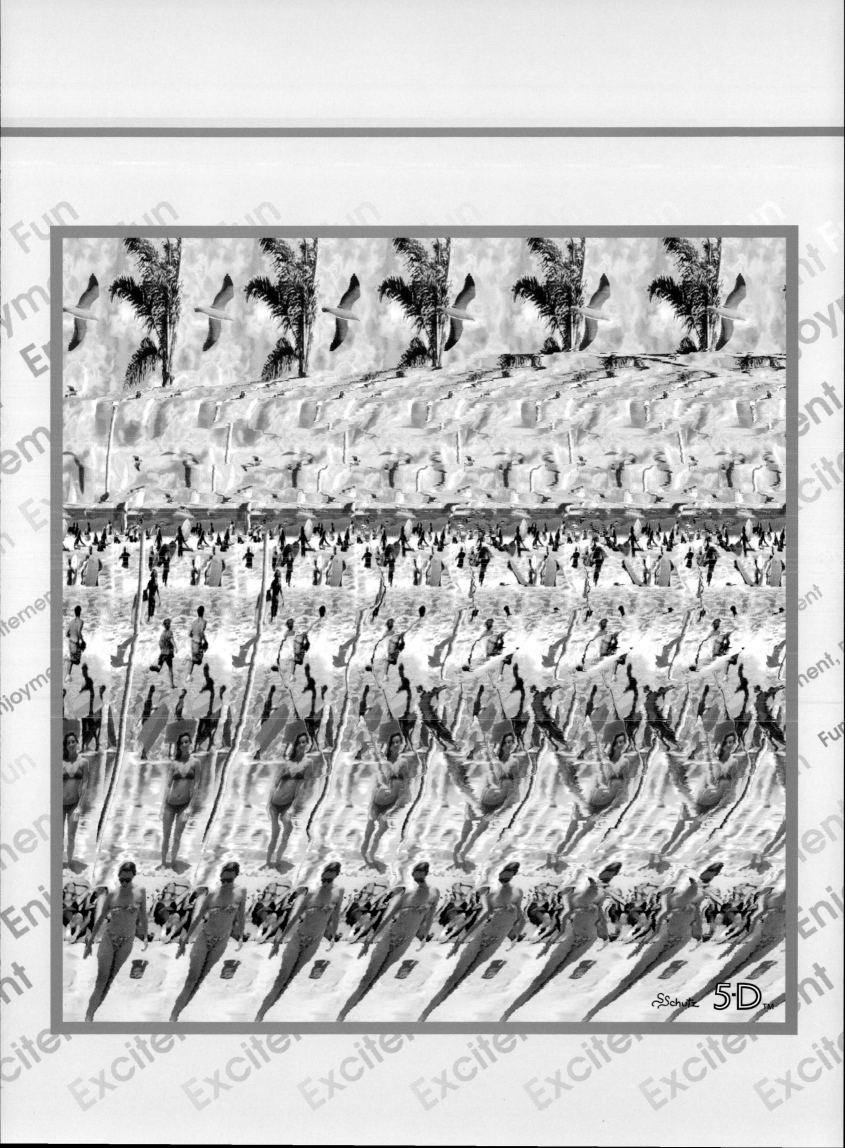

Diversity

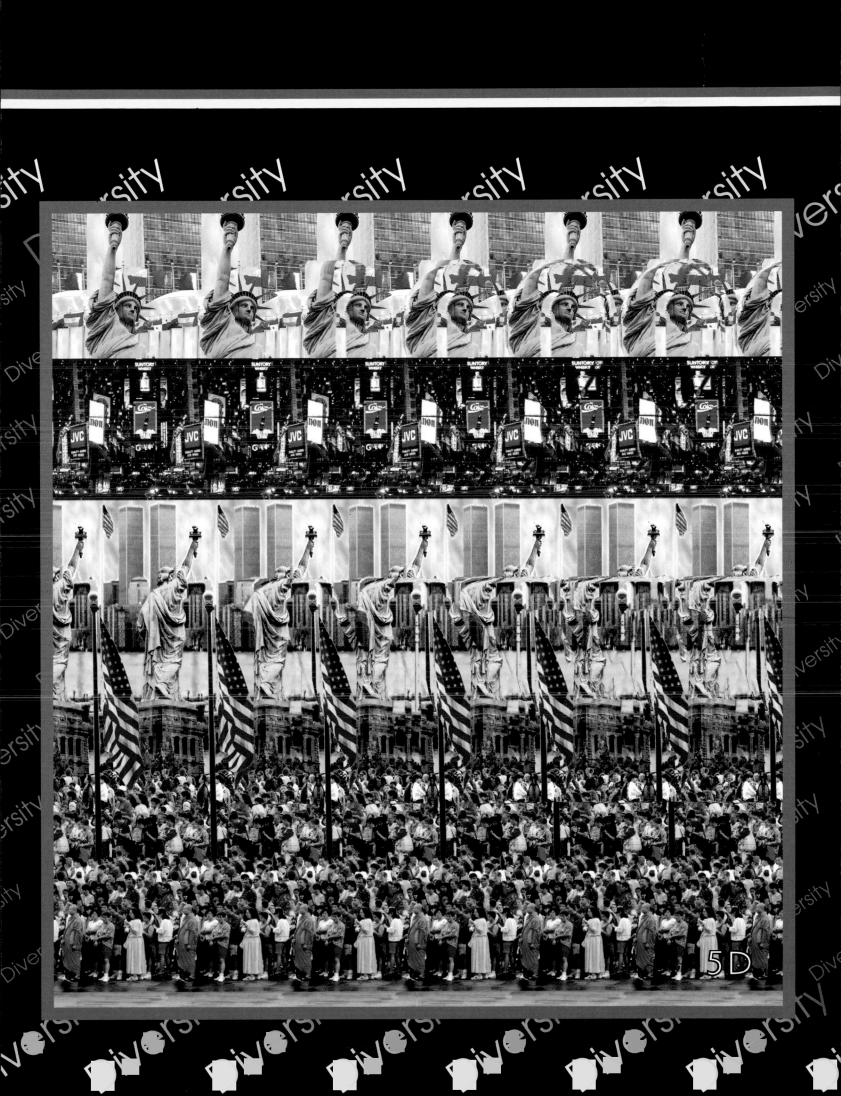

Love

5-D™ Stereogram Image: **"Love Hearts"**

5-D™ Stereogram Image: **"United Nations Building"**

Dreams can come true
if you take the time to
think about what you want in life
Get to know yourself
Find out who you are
Choose your goals carefully
Be honest with yourself
Always believe in yourself
Find interests and pursue them
Find out what is important to you
Find out what you are good at
Don't be afraid to make mistakes
Work hard to achieve successes
When things are not going right
don't give up—just try harder
Find courage inside of you to remain strong
Give yourself freedom to try out new things
Don't be so set in your ways that you can't grow
Always act in an ethical way
Laugh and have a good time
Form relationships with people you respect
Treat others as you want them to treat you
Be honest with people
Accept the truth
Speak the truth
Open yourself up to love
Don't be afraid to love
Remain close to your family
Take part in the beauty of nature
Be appreciative of all that you have
Help those less fortunate than you
Work towards peace and happiness in the world
Live life to the fullest
Create your own dreams
and follow them
until they
become a reality

— Susan Polis Schutz

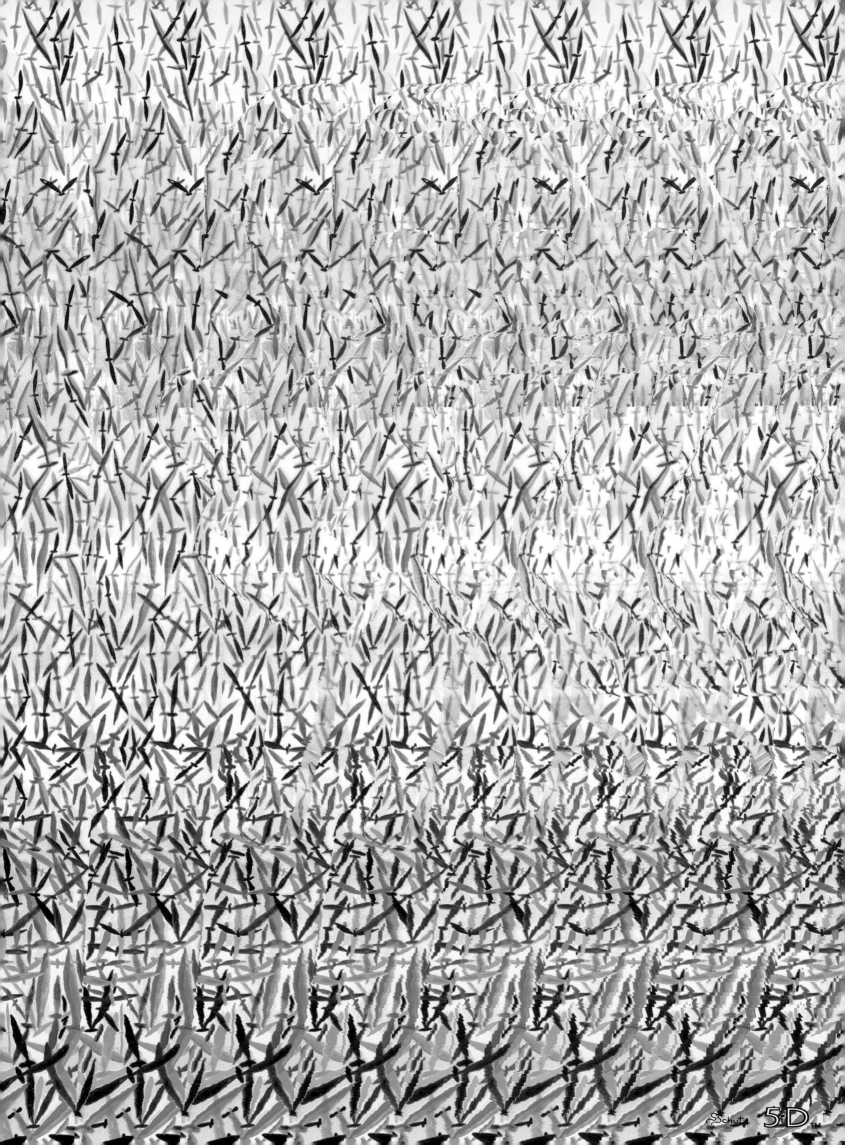

Achievement

5-D™ Stereogram Image: **"Home Run"**

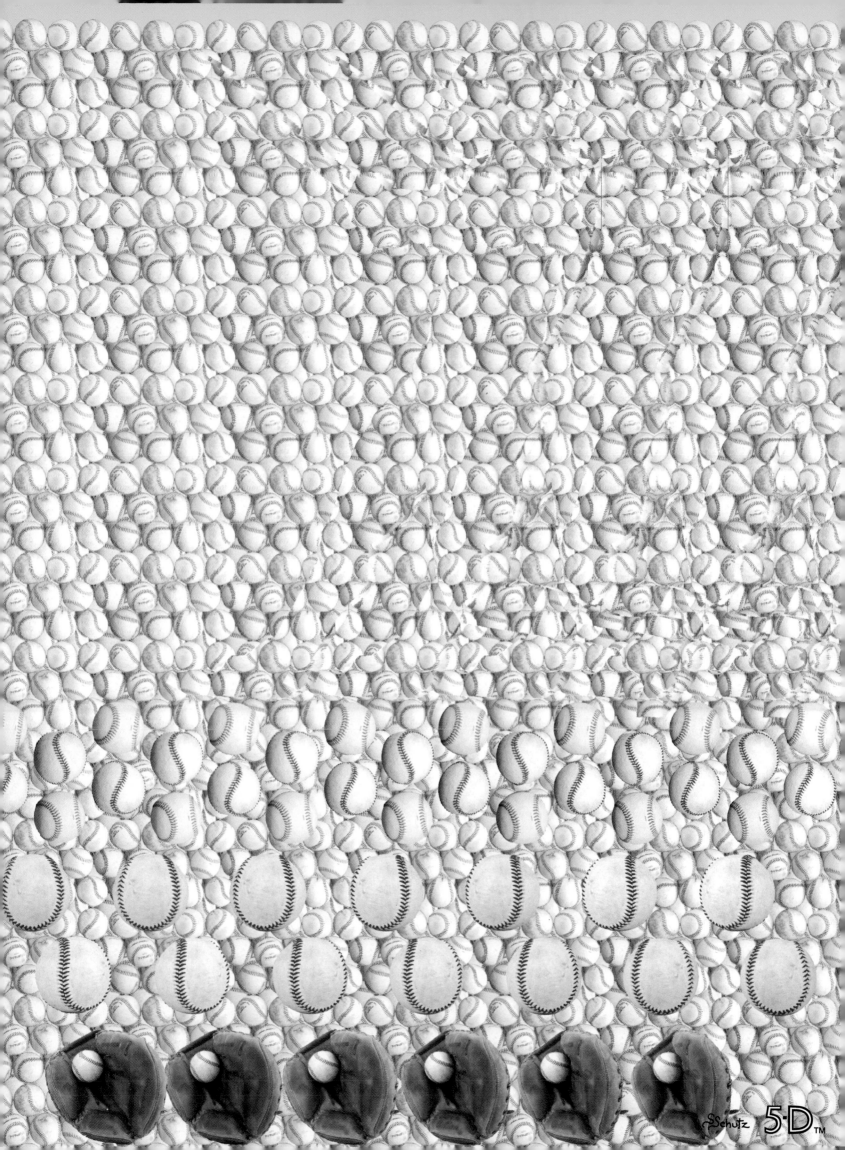

5-D™ Stereogram Image: "Song"

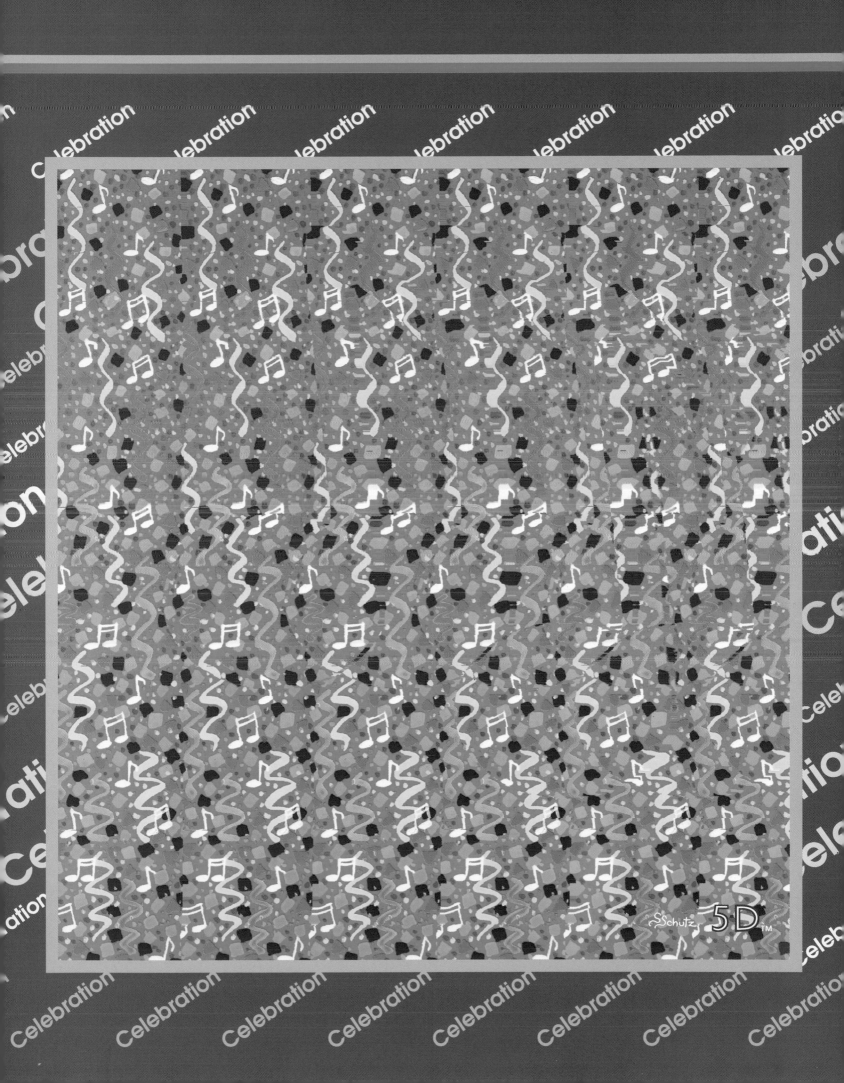

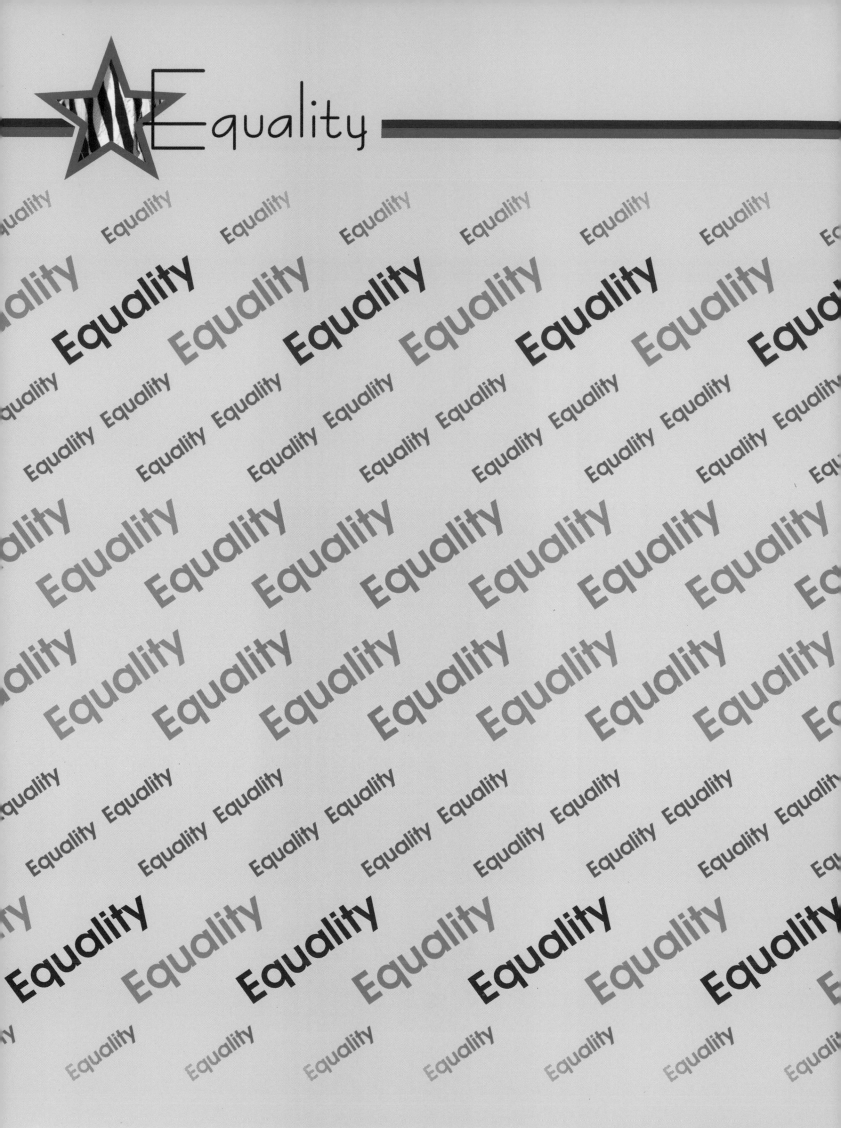

Equality

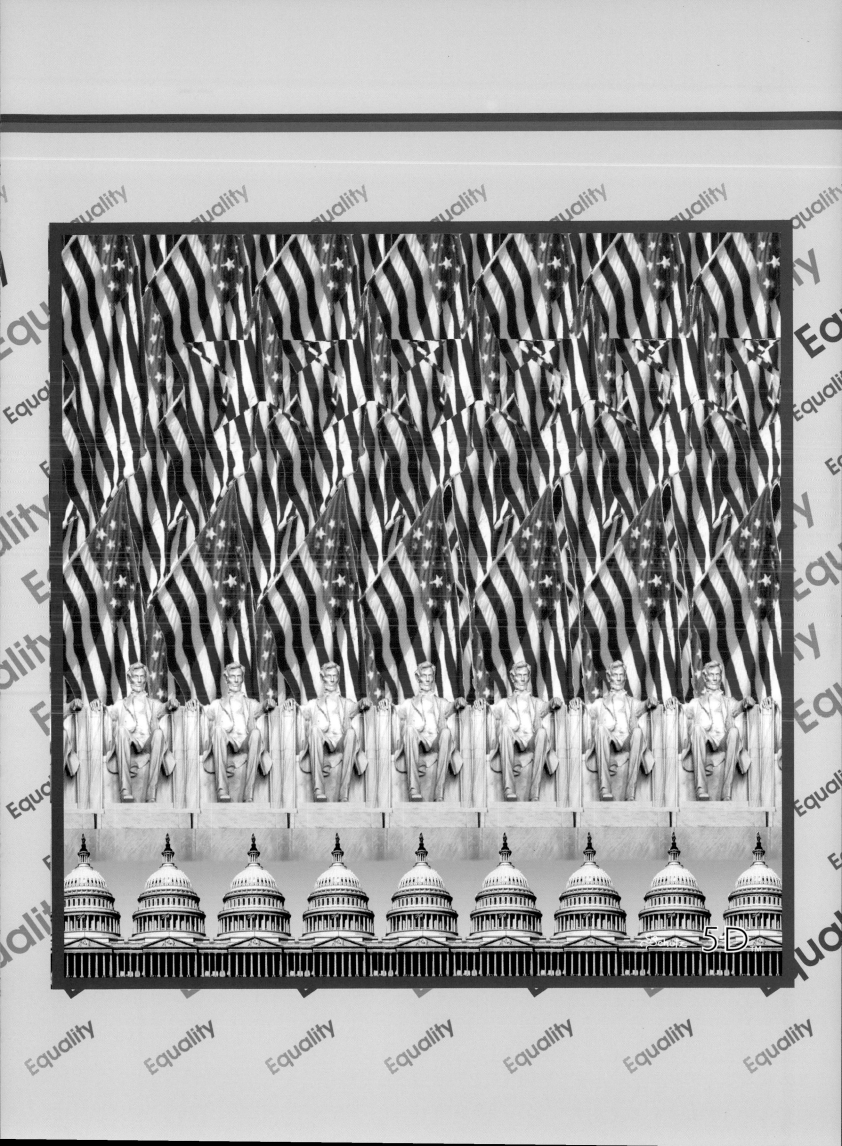

Liberty

Friendship

5-D™ Stereogram Image: **"Birds in Friendship"**

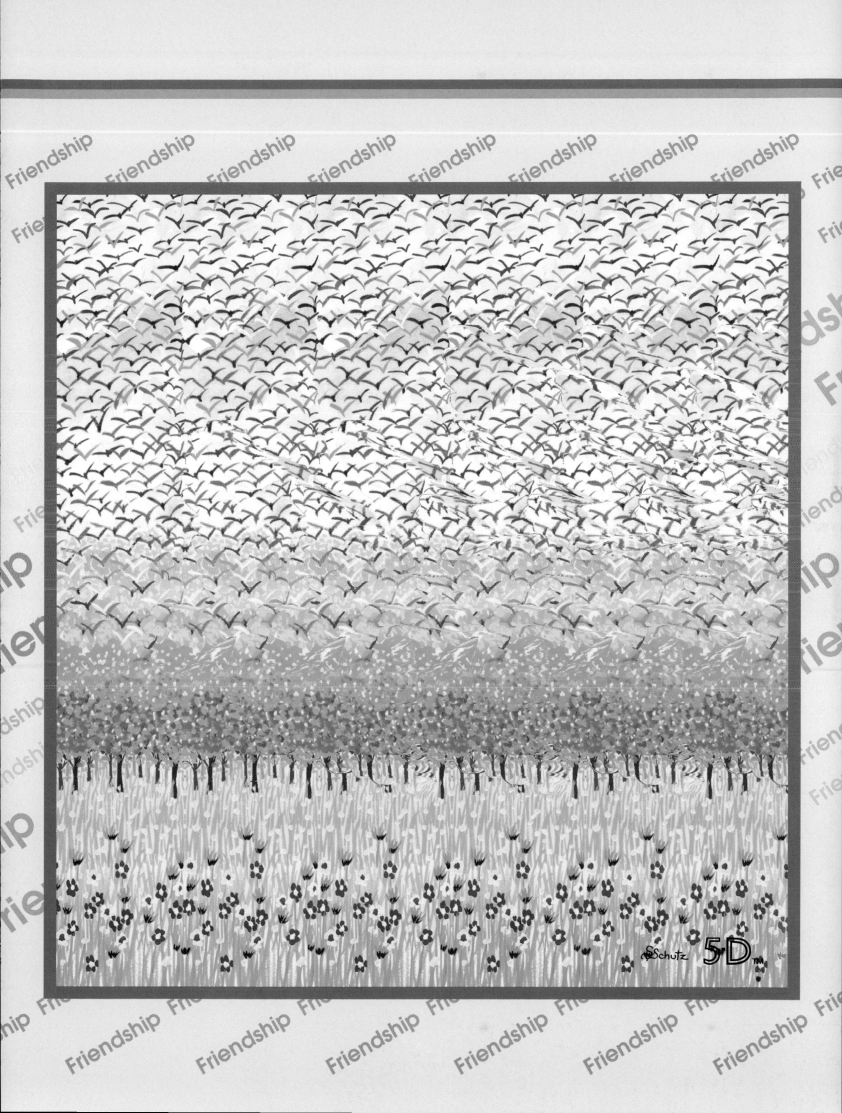

Dreams

Spirit

5-D™ Stereogram Image: **"The Song of the Wolf"**

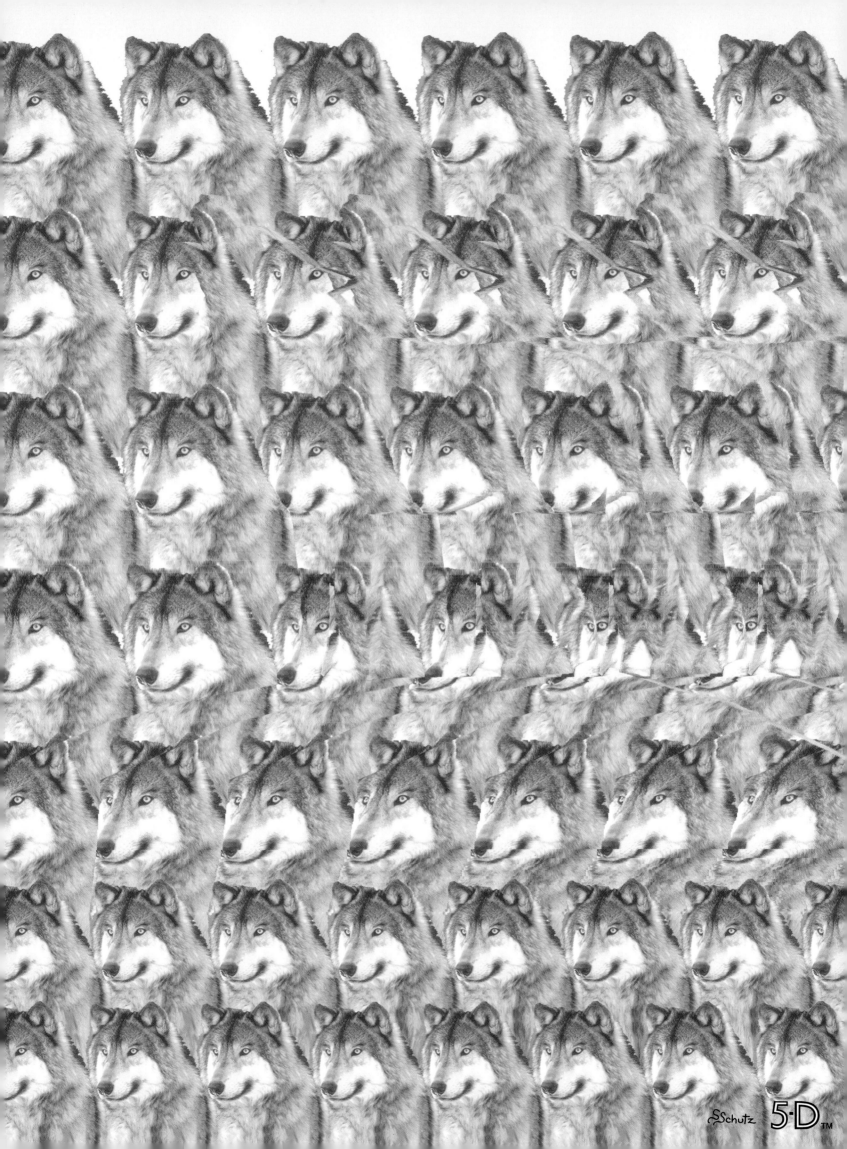

Seeing in Stereo

Stephen Schutz, Ph.D., Takes the Art of the Stereogram to a New Aesthetic Level

Recent improvements in computer technology have enabled the famous artist (and physicist) Stephen Schutz to pass a new threshold of innovation and liberate art from its prior two-dimensional limitations. "Spectacular!" says Leonard Nimoy about 5-D™ stereograms. "Beautiful and often dazzling works of art," says Dick Kreck of *The Denver Post*. And from Sheldon Aronowitz, the owner of the largest 3-D collection in the world: "Finally, a refreshing improvement in dimensional images—pictures you will find yourself getting 'lost' in—pictures that will put the word 'WOW!' back in your vocabulary."

5-D™ stereograms, Stephen Schutz's most recent artistic creation, effectively establish a genre of Multi-Dimensional art. Stereograms had their origins in 1960 when Bela Julesz developed the "random-dot stereogram" as a tool to study perceptual psychology. For the past thirty years, primitive random-dot stereograms have relied on repetitive textures to disguise hidden three-dimensional images.

Stephen Schutz's 5-D™ stereograms have successfully replaced random-dot textures with incredible artwork, which makes 5-D™ stereograms "dimensional dynamite," in the words of David Hutchison of the National Stereoscopic Association. The full-color base-art foregrounds (what everyone sees on the surface) are attractions in and of themselves. When this foreground is dramatically supplemented by a hidden image that relates and interacts with it, the exquisite result comes alive as wolves leap off the page and stars hang in a multi-layered sky. Stephen Schutz's accomplishment is a testimony to what can happen when the creative envelope of art is expanded and enhanced by the cutting edge of technology.

"Over the past few years, random-dot stereograms have been popping up all over the place. Unfortunately, most are very boring," notes 3-D collector and writer for *Stereo World* magazine, Sheldon Aronowitz. "This has all changed with the release of the Blue Mountain Arts 5-D™ stereograms developed by Dr. Stephen Schutz. In their flat format, they are works of art in their own right. When viewed in three dimensions, you will be amazed and delighted with the clarity and ingenious blending of theme. No more patterns of endless dots."

This intriguing image represents how the computer "sees" Stephen Schutz's Multi-Dimensional image that appears on page 13. The computer uses colors to designate dimensional levels; objects on the same level are of the same color. The computer then integrates these color levels with the chosen background art and transforms them into 5-D™ stereograms by applying Stephen Schutz's advanced programmed formula.

About the Artist and Author

Stephen Schutz is an artist and a physicist, a rare combination of talents emanating from the mind and heart. Enraptured at an early age with beauty and aesthetic form, Stephen pursued the paths of science and art simultaneously. He graduated from the famous High School of Music and Art in New York City, and studied physics at M.I.T. and Princeton University, where he received a Ph.D. in theoretical physics in 1970. While pursuing advanced scientific learning, Stephen continued to develop his artistic abilities at the Museum of Fine Arts in Boston.

During college, Stephen met and fell in love with the woman who was to become his equal loving partner in marriage, family, and art. In1969, Susan Polis Schutz and Stephen Schutz moved to the mountains of Colorado where Susan was a freelance writer and Stephen researched solar energy at a government research laboratory. On the weekends, they began experimenting with printing Susan's poems surrounded by Stephen's art on posters that they silk-screened in their basement. From the very start, their love of life and for one another touched a receptive chord in people everywhere. The public's discovery of the creative collaboration of Susan Polis Schutz and Stephen Schutz set the stage for a world-wide love affair with their works.

"Susan Polis Schutz remains one of the most popular poets in America today," reports the Associated Press, "and her work touches virtually everyone." Her honest and compelling poems have a universal appeal. As a frequent visitor to the bestseller lists, Susan and Stephen's books and poetry cards have touched the hearts of over 200 million people, and Susan's verse has been translated into many foreign languages. Susan is living proof that love and friendship are the universal languages, and she continues to find new ways to share her thoughts through her peaceful and inspiring poems.

As Susan's achievements have grown, so too have Stephen's. His instinctive curiosity about the way things work keeps him evolving as an artist, as a scholar, and as a person. An important part of the evolutionary process for all of us has been the computer. Stephen began working with a computer in the early 1960s when, according to Stephen, "You didn't even see the actual computer because it was tucked away somewhere in the building, taking up an entire room. Now a desktop computer can perform functions in a minute that required countless hours for the huge early machines to perform."

Because Stephen is an artist, computer whiz, and innovator, there is no one better suited to take the art of the stereogram to its next level. Combine that with the fact that it would be difficult to discover a poet with a more significant following than Susan Polis Schutz, who *TIME* magazine referred to as the "reigning star... in high-emotion." Together, Susan and Stephen Schutz's most recent books, featuring Susan's poetic messages and Stephen's 5-D$_{TM}$ stereograms, are just the latest in a series of beautiful contributions the couple has made over the past 25 years.

Photo by Jared